GOD STILL DOES MIRACLES TODAY

Colorado

Carole Arnold

ISBN 979-8-88851-591-4 (Paperback)
ISBN 979-8-88851-592-1 (Digital)

Copyright © 2023 Carole Arnold
All rights reserved
First Edition

All rights reserved. No part of this publication may be reproduced, distributed, or transmitted in any form or by any means, including photocopying, recording, or other electronic or mechanical methods without the prior written permission of the publisher. For permission requests, solicit the publisher via the address below.

Covenant Books
11661 Hwy 707
Murrells Inlet, SC 29576
www.covenantbooks.com

*To my wonderful husband, Carl
He is my friend, a very hard worker, a great father,
and my long-suffering spouse of so many years*

*Also to my two beloved sons, Vinnie and Teddy,
and my four delightful grandchildren*

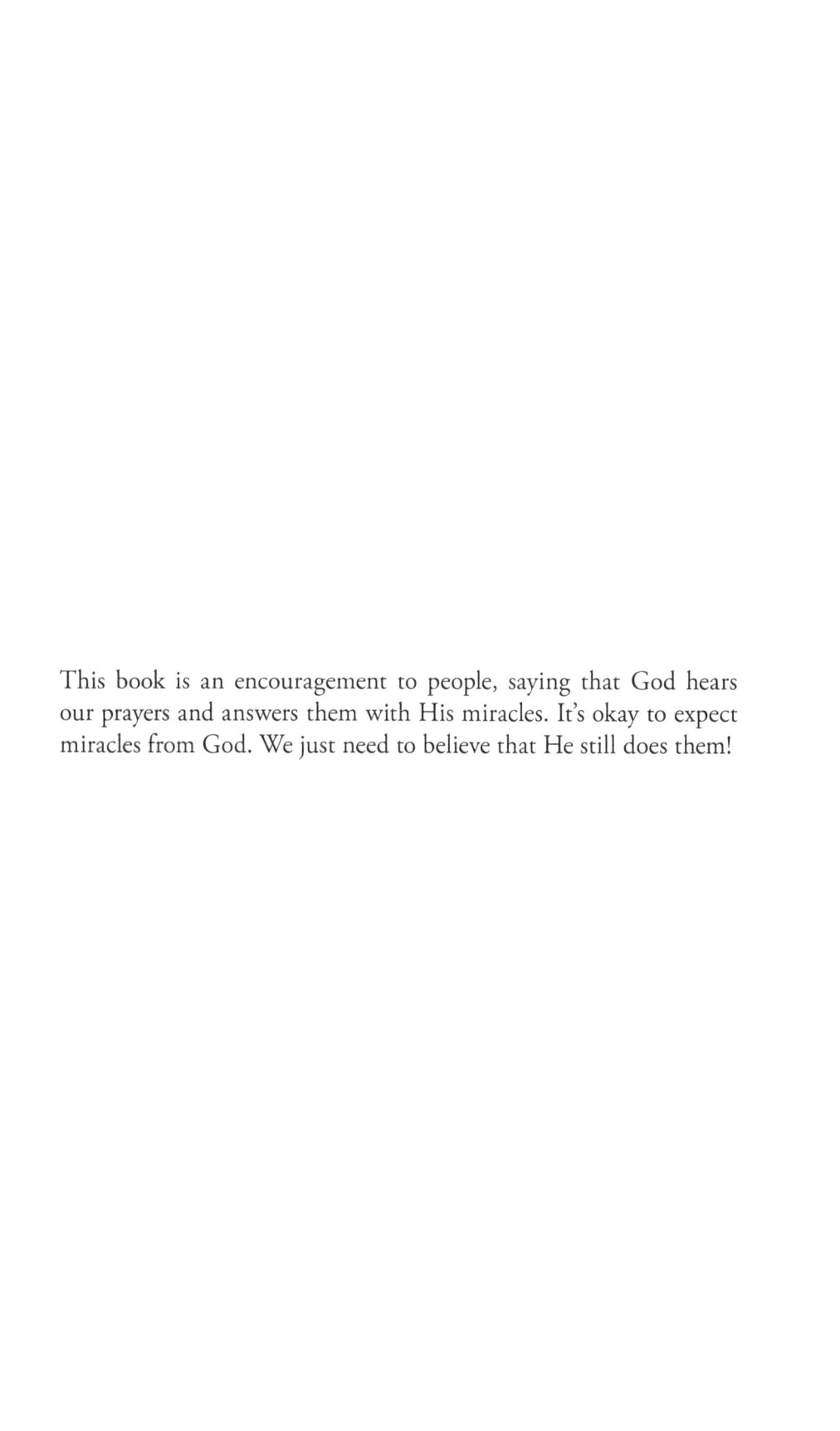

This book is an encouragement to people, saying that God hears our prayers and answers them with His miracles. It's okay to expect miracles from God. We just need to believe that He still does them!

INTRODUCTION

Whenever I watch and listen to preachers who are attempting to encourage people to serve the living God, my continuous thought has been that I wish I could tell the listening people about our "road-grader miracle" that we had received from God many years ago. This was a spectacular miracle that God performed for two people who certainly did not deserve it. We were just average joes who were trying to make life work with our own strength and wisdom. God wisely let us hit rock bottom before He finally began to bless us with His miracles. We had become so desperate that we were finally beginning to see our need of Him in our lives.

I just want to let people, especially Christians, know that we don't have to be mightily religious folks in order for God to care about us. We are all just actually casting around in the darkness, looking for hope, looking for something reliable to cling to. All that we really need to be is needy believers who have finally decided that it is absolutely necessary to start trusting God completely to give His help to us and grant us much-needed miracles.

God's miracles can be every believer's experience. This is what listening congregations need to know: God is ready and willing to help all of us. We do not have to spend gut-wrenching hours trying to find some way to get God to help us. God has asked in Genesis 18:14, "Is anything too difficult for the Lord?" The answer to that is a resounding *no*!

An everyday life, with all its ups and downs, can become a life that is full of God's miracles, and this can be every believer's experience. Yes, God is still doing miracles today. He is the same yesterday, today, and forever (Hebrews 13:8). God never changes, nor does He ever leave us or forsake us (Malachi 3:6, Hebrews 13:5). If it seems like God has left us or has never even worked in our lives, it's not true. Rather, it's us who have not engaged with Him or who have wandered away from Him. God waits for us to invite Him to take care of us. He will even scatter bread crumbs (meaning, He allows circumstances to ensnare us) in order to catch our attention. But we must finally give in and follow His bread crumbs to Him for His help. God awaits our prayer requests, then responds to them.

CHAPTER 1

Who could have ever guessed that a huge road grader would be God's spectacular answer to a desperate prayer? Nevertheless, that's the way that God does things—His own way, His unique way, a way that can't be second-guessed or duplicated by people. It's because of the splendid miracles that God has done for our family—a family, by the way, that is just a bunch of average joes—that I want to write this book.

Recently, as America struggles with overwhelming unbelief in God and preachers are trying so hard to encourage Americans to turn to or return to God, I am constantly being urged by God to speak about His miraculous miracles in our lives. This would help people get the encouragement that they need. This encouragement should lift the spirits of more average joes just like us who need to be assured that God is indeed still mightily at work in today's world. We merely have to ask God for His help, believing that He hears us and that He wants to respond to us. He is never too far away to hear and answer us with one of His glorious miracles.

I need to tell you who the "we" that I am talking about in this book are. My husband, Carl, and I have been married for forty-five years now. This was neither a joyous nor a practical marriage. In the first place, I am eleven years older than Carl. I have always been a Republican because I am a farmer's daughter. Carl has always been a Democrat because he and his family are union members. My family is a nondrinking family. Furthermore, I love to travel, ride motorcycles, dance joyously, and live life in a wonderfully spontaneous manner. On the other hand, Carl is a stay-at-home kind of guy. He is scared of motorcycles, absolutely abhors dancing, and lives his life according to a scheduled daily routine. To Carl, the word *spontaneous* is a horrifying threat to a well-ordered life. His idea of a good time is to go fishing. Most of all, because his family are all union members, drinking is just natural to Carl.

How in the world did Carl and I ever think that marriage could work for us? Well, I was thirty years old and pregnant, and Carl was twenty-one years old and drunk! Also, since I had been raised in a teetotalist family, I actually did not recognize that Carl was an alcoholic and that I was marrying into a hard time.

It was 1975. Carl and I met each other at the company where we both worked in, in Denver, Colorado. I was the new head of the service department, and Carl was the head of the warehouse. When we crossed paths, the sparks flew! I first went out to the warehouse to get some parts for a service customer, and it was there that I first saw Carl. He had his back to me and was standing on top of some garage door springs, and I liked what I saw! My heart leapt, and I said to myself, "Wow, I need to get to know this guy." Shortly after that, Carl came into the service department to arrange a service for one of his warehouse customers. When he saw me, he was looking at a pretty, buxom, platinum-blond lady. He thought to himself, *Wow, I need to get to know this lady.* And so it began. Very soon, Carl asked me out on our first date.

In the second place, we had both assumed that we were both approximately twenty-five years old—just perfect for each other. To me, Carl looked older than he was, and to Carl, I looked younger than I was. As it turned out, at that time, I was twenty-eight years old, and he was seventeen years old! We dated for a couple of months before it began to dawn on me that we just were not operating in the same age group. We simply didn't seem to have the age-appropriate lifestyles that we expected of each other.

We finally discovered that we had an eleven-year age difference. What a shock that was to both of us! It occurred to me that Carl was my boy toy and that I was his cougar. But it was already too late as we were both hooked on each other by then. Carl was a drunk, and I had already been married and divorced three times. But those facts didn't seem to present any problems that we couldn't deal with.

Besides, we had already "fallen in love," so the obvious problems didn't faze us.

After a couple of years together, I discovered that I was pregnant. I opted for an abortion, but Carl was having none of that. He said, "Nobody kills my baby!" Therefore, in spite of the many obvious obstacles to the possibility of a good marriage, we got married in 1977. I was thirty years old, and Carl was nineteen years old. (I am still embarrassed to admit this!) Immediately things began going downhill from then on. Before marriage, we had wanted to be together. After marriage, we were forced to be together!

I had been raised in a modestly Christian Methodist family. Carl had been raised in a mixed—thus, barely Christian—family. One of Carl's parents was a nonpracticing Catholic, and the other one was a nonpracticing Presbyterian. I had some knowledge of the Bible, and I had always assumed that I was a Christian because my parents were Christians. Carl had some knowledge of Christianity, but the constant bickering of his parents over religion left him cold toward God. However, we both knew that there was a God who loved us and that we believed in Him. In fact, Carl had crashed his car on a mountain road when he was sixteen years old and had died. He had found himself up in the air at about the height of the telephone poles, looking down on his own body, as the rescue workers were pulling it out of his smashed car! Then Carl was suddenly back in his body and alive, looking *up* at his rescuers! He had only been a little physically damaged. His car had been totally demolished. The fact that he had been drunk at the time probably saved his life. (See what I mean about how God leaves bread crumbs leading to Himself?)

We got married in my Methodist church, which we had both attended on Christmases and on Easters. We were "C and E-ers"—Christians who only went to church on the two major Christian holidays. That was how we attempted to satisfy God's demands on us. The details of our early years together were pretty average for two people of our foolish inclinations, with lots of fighting interspersed in them. I had always been looking for love in all of the wrong places, and Carl had always been a drinker, because that's what union men do. (Carl was not a mean drunk. No, he was just passed out most of the time after he started drinking. I was grateful for that!)

Sadly, three months after we got married, I miscarried our baby. Boy, that was a shock to us. We had gotten married in order to provide a home for this baby, but now there was no baby to legitimize this marriage, which was already beginning to fail anyway.

Carl and Carole at their wedding, 1977

CHAPTER 2

Because my body had so prepared itself to have a baby, I was all in, trying to get pregnant again. My baby doctor told me that I could certainly try to get pregnant again and that I could very well be successful in carrying the next baby to full term. So I begged Carl to make me another baby, and he zealously set to work on that project! Our beautiful son, Ted, was born the next year, in February 1979. I was thirty-two years old, and Carl was twenty-one.

I already had my first son, who is ten years older than Ted. His name is Vinnie, and he was living with his father at the time. I was now the proud mother of two fine sons. Vinnie finally came to live near Carl, Ted, and me when he was eighteen years old. He and Ted are happy half brothers. Blessedly, both of my sons had given their hearts to the Lord. To me, these are two of God's many miracles that He has done for me. But I digress.

I have two sisters, both of whom had become born-again believers some time ago. They constantly nagged me to give my life to Jesus, but I thought that I was already a Christian, so I just ignored them. Meanwhile, my marriage was definitely already tanking. Carl drank steadily, and we fought constantly. One day, out of the blue, Carl asked me for a divorce. That was such a shock to me. *Nobody leaves me*, I thought. *I do the leaving.* It made me so mad that I instantly became bound and determined to save the marriage even though I had been considering a divorce myself. But I was really not relishing a fourth divorce, and I really did not want to have my second son be in yet another one of my custody battles. (These are two more of God's bread crumbs again!)

Nevertheless, Carl packed up and went to live at his father's house. He came over to our house from time to time to take care of the lawn and, of course, lay down the law to me. He would not allow me to talk to him, and he refused to listen to me if I tried to talk to him. Carl said that I must go rent an apartment for myself and that when I had one (which better be soon), he would come back to our house to live. Furthermore, Carl insisted that he would keep Teddy. This was the last straw for me!

I had already lost my first son to his father. I simply was not willing to lose my second son to his father. Alas, though, I was out of options. Here I was thirty-four years old and already heading for my fourth divorce. I didn't have a job. I didn't have any money. I had no intention of following Carl's instructions, but I had nowhere to turn and no one to turn to. I was at my wit's end, desperate for solutions. All I could do was go sit on the end of our bed, crying my eyes out. I sobbed out, "God, if You are really there, please show me."

A voice clearly replied to me, "Get your radio."

I instantly knew the radio that God was referring to. It was an old gray plastic radio, very obsolete. I hadn't seen it for years. Even so, I got up, zombied myself into the den, and opened the closet door. And there was that old radio sitting right up front on the shelf! I was shocked yet again, but I took that radio back into the bedroom and plugged it in. The radio was blaring out some loud, head-banging music. Suddenly the music went silent, and then that same voice that had sent me to the radio boomed out of the radio, "Ask and it shall be given to you, seek and you shall find, knock and it shall be opened to you." This is a Bible verse (Matthew 7:7 and Luke 11:9), but I didn't know that because I had never read my Bible. I then unplugged that old radio and put it back in the den closet. I have *never* seen that radio again! These are more of God's glorious miracles done for me.

The only thing that I knew to do then was call one of my sisters and ask her if she knew if that was God talking to me and how one asked, sought, and knocked. She said that I should immediately get myself to church. She suggested a church that was not far down the road from my house. I hustled myself to that church the following Wednesday evening. It turned out to be Pastor Tom Stipe's Calvary Chapel church. At the end of the service, Pastor Stipe prayed a sinner's prayer, and I fully gave my heart to Jesus at that time.

I started praying constantly. God told me to obey my husband's rules, so I went out and found an apartment to rent. I used the grocery money to pay the down payment on the first month's rent. However, under my breath, I told God that if He didn't save my marriage, then I would fight back and sue Carl for everything he was worth, union retirement and all! After all, Carl was the "drunk," and I was the "good guy"!

The next evening, Carl came over late at night to tell me his terms of the divorce and to arrange for me to leave Teddy, who was now two years old, with him. I muttered to God, "This is Your last chance to save this marriage. If I am actually poised to leave tomorrow morning, I will counter Carl's terms, tell him *my* terms, and begin my own divorce proceedings!"

God whispered back, "Just obey your husband!"

Carl and I were in the dark living room with only the kitchen light on. Teddy was in bed, asleep. Carl was pacing around at the far end of the living room, in the dark, and I could hardly see him. I was sitting in a chair at the near end of the living room, so the kitchen light was shining only on me. I was seething but praying silently as Carl yelled instructions at me. I just kept saying, "Yes, dear." Carl was drunk at the time—as usual. Suddenly I saw a very narrow beam of light momentarily shine down from the living room ceiling, shining a pinpoint of light right on Carl's head. Instantly, Carl stopped pacing, turned toward me, and said in a perfectly sober voice, "What am I doing? I don't want a divorce!" Then the little pinpoint of light disappeared.

I said, "Well, I certainly don't want a divorce either!"

And there was another shocking, miraculous miracle of God!

After a bit, Carl told me that he was going to go to sleep in "his" bed and that I should sleep on the living room couch. He said that we would talk again in the morning. Carl went down the hall to our bedroom, and I got a blanket and pillow out of the linen closet and lay down on the couch.

I was very mad that Carl had been treating me so badly but was even more grateful to God for saving my marriage. As I settled in, God asked me, "What are you doing on the couch?"

I whispered back, "I'm doing what You told me to do. I'm obeying my husband."

God said, "Get up and go to bed with Carl."

I got up, went into the bedroom, and crawled into bed with Carl.

Carl said, "What are you doing here?"

I said, "I came to make up with you."

Then we spent the whole night making up!

The next morning, since we were still married, Carl moved back home, and we went on as before—both of us in love but miserable. I never went back to the apartment that I had rented, so we lost that grocery money.

Carl, Carole, and Ted (age three)

However, I was now a Jesus-loving Christian anxious to please Him *and* Carl. God had proved to me that He was there, and I was hungry for more of His miracles. I began to pray day and night, many times lying on my face on the bedroom floor for hours. I went to church twice a week. I went to Marilyn Hickey's Happy Church every Friday night, where we all prayed and sang songs all night with Marilyn's husband, Wally Hickey. Usually, I took Teddy and a few of his little toys with me, and he would play with his toys on the plush pew until he fell asleep. Sometimes Teddy and I stayed all night long. Carl did not mind all of the time that I was spending at various churches, as long as I didn't bug him to go.

One night, a sweet Black lady who I didn't know and had never heard of my marriage problems came over to me. She handed me a small piece of a red bandana. She said that she had prayed over this "prayer cloth," that I should put it under my husband's pillow, and that he would get saved soon because of her and my faith that God would see to it. How did that lady know about my marriage? That was a whole new concept to me, but I dutifully did so. I put the prayer cloth between the mattress and the box springs, though, so that Carl wouldn't find it.

I didn't find out until some years later that this was very biblical. The apostle Paul had prayed over cloths, and God had used those cloths as touch points to perform healing miracles for people. (Acts 19:11–12). (PS: Carl did eventually get saved, but I had forgotten about that red prayer cloth by then. I had found it between the mattresses a long time later! Read James 5:16.)

Meanwhile, Carl stayed home, drinking beer, watching TV, and sleeping in his recliner. (He still naps in his recliner today!) I never asked or pushed Carl to get saved because God had told me that I should just continue to obey Carl while I continue on my journey with God. Carl was okay with Teddy and me going to church so much because it left him free to live life at his own leisure in the evenings and weekends. Carl never missed a day's work, but he worked hard, and then he came home and drank hard. He still has never missed a day's work, and I am very impressed with his work ethic and thankful.

CHAPTER 3

Carl has one older brother (Howard), a younger sister (Bethie), and two younger brothers (Dean and Danny). All of them had had plenty of youthful troubles by the time I met them. My favorite brother-in-law is Dean, who is Carl's first younger brother. Dean was also the most troubled and rebellious of the five kids. Perhaps that is why I identify so well with him—because he was just like me!

One day, about two weeks after I had gotten saved and certainly well before I knew much about God and how to witness for Him to people, I was driving down the street past Howard's house. Just as I was driving by, I saw Dean walking away from Howard's house. I pulled the car over and asked Dean if he would like a ride to wherever he was going. Dean accepted and got in my car. He was going to Bethie's house, where he lived, and it wasn't very far away. As we rode along, Dean was grumbling about how miserable his life was. Suddenly my mouth blurted out, "It sounds like you need Jesus, Dean!" My words shocked both of us. Dean did not know that I was a Christian, and I didn't know that I could present Jesus to anyone.

Dean answered, "I do?" So I said that I guessed that he probably did need the Lord. We rode along in silence after that, both of us contemplating what had just been said.

When we got to Bethie's house, Dean mumbled his thanks and his goodbye to me, jumped out of the car, and raced into Bethie's house. Of course, Dean, who was nineteen years old then, never told me that he had decided to go back to Bethie's house, get a gun that he had stashed away, go down to the basement, and shoot himself. However, because I had told him that he needed Jesus, he laid the gun on his bed and flung himself onto the basement floor, crying out to God for help. The result was that Dean spent most of three days and nights lying prone on that floor, getting to know Jesus. When he finally got up, Dean got into the shower and baptized himself in Jesus's name! Obviously, this was a God-ordained meeting between Dean and me set up by God to save Dean's life. Of course, I didn't know that at the time. I know now that God had not just saved me for myself; He had a whole other family in mind when He intervened in my life! (Here's another example of God's laying down bread crumbs and working wonderful miracles for us.) He just needed me to be His ambassador to Dean while believing that God still does miracles.

Carl's first younger brother, Dean

CAROLE ARNOLD

Carole's two sisters: older sister Barbi and younger sister Cathryn

Shortly thereafter, Dean called Carl and me on the phone and told us his story. I was just flabbergasted. And Carl? Well, he was a little drunk and not much impressed. But from that moment on, Dean and I became more than just in-laws. We became Christian buddies and churchgoing pals. Dean got a Bible, and he and I started going to Wednesday-evening church services every week. What wonderful times we had together. We are still having those good times these forty years later.

Dean even got an urge to preach the gospel on the streets of downtown Denver. I went along with him occasionally even though this seemed to be a rather scary endeavor and, therefore, a downright foolish thing to do. I always took my tape player along. I would sit on benches and softly play Christian music while Dean preached to the drunks and the loiterers in the streets. Dean continued doing it for a few years, although I quit going along after a while because it was just too scary to me. What funny stories Dean would often tell us about his experiences on the streets of Denver.

In the meantime, Dean had an upcoming trial to go to for impersonating his little brother, Danny, on a driver's license, which could have sent him to jail for five years. Dean was all prayed up to get the courage to face this trial. He stopped at our house on the way to court, and Carl and I prayed with him. Amazingly, he was soon right back to our house. He said that when he got to court, the judge didn't know who Dean was and had no information on any Dean Arnold that was supposed to face him in court. He cleared Dean's name and sent Dean off a free man! We praised God together, guessing that God had sent big angels with big erasers to deal with this matter!

Every Wednesday evening, Dean and I would come back to my house after evening church services for a cup of coffee. Carl would be asleep in his recliner in the dark living room. Dean and I would talk quietly but excitedly about the wonderful sermons and prayer services that we had just enjoyed. Carl would have already put Teddy to bed and then retired to the living room, beer in hand, to watch TV and fall asleep in his recliner. Dean and I would try to always talk quietly even though our excitement was quite exuberant. We just didn't want to disturb Carl and make him mad.

One evening, Carl's voice came booming out of the dark living room. He was drunkenly yelling, "I want my *own* Bible so I can find out for myself if what you two are saying is true!" Talk about yet another shocking miracle from God! Dean and I were just floored. We had never bugged Carl to get saved, of course. Dean was a little intimidated by Carl, and I was simply trying to be obedient to God and obey Carl by never telling him that he needed to get saved too, which he had made perfectly clear to me. Dean and I meekly answered, "Okay!"

There was a small Christian bookstore not far from our house, and I just happened to know the lady who worked there. The next morning, I called this lady up and told her that my husband wanted a Bible and that we would be going to her store on Saturday morning to buy one. I asked her if she could pick out about three easy-to-read beginner Bibles and have them on the counter before we got there. She agreed to do that. Of course, when we got there that Saturday morning, Carl sauntered in, acting like he knew what he was doing. He swaggered around the store for a little bit and then swaggered up to the counter. He asked the lady if she knew of any easy-to-read Bibles.

She said, "Well, yes, I do. I even happen to have three good ones lying right here on the counter."

Carl paged through them, then picked out a large-print, red-letter King James Bible. He still has this Bible after all these years, although we both read New American Standard Bibles now.

Carl took his new Bible home and started reading through it slowly now and then. After three more months, having read halfway through the Old Testament and having started at Genesis 1:1, Carl gave his heart to Jesus! What a joy that was. This is not to say that he had quit drinking yet, but he said that he was thinking about it. I prayed and prayed privately for God to help Carl quit. I even promised God that if He got Carl to stop drinking, then I would never drink an alcoholic beverage myself again.

One day, after a short while, Carl came into the house from the backyard. He slammed his beer can and his cigarettes down on the kitchen table and said that he was done with both of them. He has never drunk or smoked again. I have also kept my promise to God, and I do not ever drink either. My grateful heart could just never go back on my promise to God. Mark 9:23 says that Jesus said, "All things are possible to him who believes." Furthermore, Jesus said in Matthew 20:21, "If you have faith as a mustard seed, you shall say to this mountain, 'Move from here to there,' and it shall move; and nothing will be impossible to you." Also, 1 John 3:21–22 says, "Whatever we ask we receive from Him, because we keep His commandments and do the things that are pleasing in His sight." Carl has read this Bible through every year from then on.

In the meantime, Dean led his sister, Bethie, to the Lord; and I led Carl's second younger brother, Danny, to the Lord. All of us have tried to lead the oldest brother, Howard, to the Lord for over forty years, but he is just not interested. However, Howard, too, has read his whole Bible through, so he knows what it says. Carl's father never got saved, although Carl, Dean, and Danny—all three—witnessed to him several times. Gary, their father, recently died Catholic but unsaved. Carl led his mother to Jesus on her deathbed. She had always believed in God, but she had never given her heart to the Lord. While she was in the hospital, dying, Carl had gone to visit her.

Carl asked her if she wanted to have her own mansion in heaven, and she cried, "Yes, I do!" Our pastor was there with Carl, and all three of us prayed together for her salvation. She died shortly afterward. We are very happy that she is waiting for us in heaven.

CHAPTER 4

One summer weekend, some short time before Carl found Jesus, he and I decided to take Teddy and go camping in our little trailer along the Colorado River, up in the Rocky Mountains. Carl worked on a swing shift, so our weekends were always three days long. There weren't many people in our camping spot; but they had all left after two days, while Carl, Teddy, and I stayed for our third day.

Now, when you drive into that camping spot down in a small valley along the river, the little road is hard-packed-down dirt, an easy drive. However, it had rained all night long on the second night that we were there alone. Since we couldn't get outside to fish or hike on the third day, Carl devoted his time to drinking. He was fairly drunk by the time that we hooked the trailer up to his old green truck to leave. I only say this in order to explain that Carl wasn't thinking clearly at the time. We were out of food and diapers for Teddy, and we had too little money to go into town some short way away to buy food and diapers. Besides that, we needed to get home in time for Carl to go to work that Monday evening. So we barreled out of our camping spot in the trees and onto the river road.

But, whoa, that hard dirt road had been turned into thick black river mud by the rain. Instantly the truck and trailer sank up to the floorboards of both vehicles and into some truly gnarly, gooey, bottom-of-the-river-type mud! There was no way that we would be moving even another inch now. Also, since the other campers had left the day before, we were all alone; there was no one around to help us in any way. Furthermore, we had no money to hire someone to come and haul us out even if Carl did hike out to find help. What a terrible crisis it was that had just overcome us—no money, no food, no diapers, and 110 miles back to home. This was way before the days of cellphones, so we were totally on our own!

Carl got out of the truck and was stomping around in the mud and kicking the truck, cussing up a storm. I sat in the truck with Teddy, praying. I prayed, "Oh Lord, only something as big as Your hand coming down out of heaven could lift this truck and trailer out of the mud and haul us out of here! But I know that won't happen, so whatever can we do?"

At that very moment, a *huge* road grader came straight down the side of the hill from the highway over across the little valley from us. He did not bother to come around on the road; he just went down the hillside. He headed directly toward us. When he wheeled very close to our truck, he yelled that he could pull us out of the mud. Well, good grief, he certainly *could* do that because his wheels were at least two times taller than our truck (as big as God's hand?)! I told God, "Well, short of *Your* hand, that grader certainly will do!" Carl had a big chain in our truck, so he attached one end to our truck and threw the other end to the guy in the road grader.

In no time flat, the guy hauled us down the little road and up the hill to the highway. We were just stunned. I was thanking and praising the Lord the whole way. Carl was glum, embarrassed, crabby, and shocked to soberness. By the time that we got to the top of the hill on that muddy dirt road, Carl had found a few dollars in his wallet. As the guy was unhooking from us, Carl jumped out of the truck to take our bit of money to the guy. But that sweet man refused the money, saying that he couldn't possibly take it. Then he told us his story.

He said that he was the supervisor of a road repair crew and he was in his pickup truck driving towards a highway repair job that he and his crew were working on. He said that, mind you, he was not a religious man but that a voice had very clearly told him to get back to his small town, get his road grader, and drive it all the way back from town to the Colorado River Valley campground. The voice told him that he would know what to do when he got there. He said that although he had never bothered about God, he knew who the voice was and that he'd best do as he had been clearly told to do!

"Okay," we said. "Thank you so very much."

"Don't thank me," he said. "I just did what I was told to do!" Then he rumbled on down the road, as stunned as we were.

This meant that God was already working out His answer to my prayer *before* we had ever hooked our truck up to our trailer to leave the campground. We knew this because the guy was already several miles down the highway toward his job when God got him to go all the way back to the town to get his road grader. Also, everyone knows how slowly a road grader moves when driving down the road, especially if they've ever been stuck driving behind one. Furthermore, we had just sunken into the mud when the grader showed up at the top of the hill. So God already had the guy driving back and forth before we ever got stuck. Now isn't that a beautiful miracle? Unfortunately, Carl wasn't nearly as impressed as I was because he was not ready yet to concede that he needed God too.

This picture is a good example of how big the road grader was

I have one other camping miracle to tell even though there were many over time. Carl, Teddy, and I decided to go camping with Dean and his wife, whom he had married recently. We were going to meet my sister and her husband in central Colorado to camp together for the weekend in the mountains. Before we got to the mountains, however, we had to drive quite a long way through the bare and wide-open plains. At one point, we had to stop both cars to get gas. While Carl and Dean were filling the cars with gas, I went to Dean's car to chat with Jan. I asked her how their trip was going. Jan said that it wasn't going too well because Dean had been fighting his usual emotional demons along the way. Carl and I knew that Dean still had not fully recovered from his youthful misadventures, but we didn't know that he was having such mental battles. I told Jan that I would be praying for her and Dean as we continued driving toward the mountains.

While Carl drove, I was silently praying very hard for Dean. As I prayed, the palms of my hands were beginning to feel like they were on fire. I knew in my heart that God wanted me to lay my hands on Dean's head while asking God to cleanse Dean's demons away. Sure enough, God gave me a small vision of a couple of trees, both of which were very tall but had no foliage on them until the very tops of both trees. Also, these trees bent across each other at their tops. This is biblical. Read Acts 2:17–18 and 1 Corinthians 12:1, for instance. I realized that God wanted us to find those trees and stop under them and me to lay hands on Dean's head and pray for him. This is very biblical. See Mark 16:17–18, where Jesus instructed us to do this very thing.

I pointed out to God that we were out on the plains, where there were no trees, least of all any that looked like coconut palms, and what would coconut palms be doing in Colorado anyway? Besides, I told God, my hands were already burning, and I didn't know if I could stand the pain and hold out much longer in order to find the trees in the vision. God just told me to keep praying as Carl kept driving. I had mentioned my vision to Carl and said that we needed to find trees and that my hands were burning, but he wasn't interested in such "dumb stuff."

Finally, we began climbing up into the mountains. Carl was looking for the spot where my sister had told us to meet them while I was desperately looking for those two coconut palms. Carl said that he was beginning to think that I was going as crazy as Dean was acting! Shortly, we came to a place where we could pull over in a lovely forest spot under some pine trees. It even looked like a nice camping place, but we were sure that this was not the place that my sister had said to meet them at. However, I leapt out of the truck, raced back to Dean's car (which he had parked behind our truck), and dragged Dean out of his car to get under two close-together pine trees. I grabbed Dean's head and started praying for him while he stood there, dumbfounded. Out of my mouth came the words "You are already clean because of the word which I have spoken to you." Wow! Where did that come from? (I still didn't know my Bible very well, so when I discovered this verse, John 15:3, some time later on, I was stunned yet again.) Dean fell onto the ground under those two trees and cried. My hands quit burning.

In the next minutes, surprisingly, my sister and her husband drove around a small curve just ahead of where we were parked, saw us, and pulled in by us. They had been driving around, looking for us, because we had not yet arrived at the right place where they had been waiting for us. They had just come across us by chance because we were even on the wrong highway! We all decided that this was actually a fine place to camp.

We settled into this nice little place, then built a campfire and made and ate some dinner. After that, I decided that I needed to take a little walk by myself to ponder the day's events. As I walked around that little curve in the road that my sister had come around, I saw those very two trees that God had shown me in my vision out on the plains! They were actually two tall pine trees with no foliage on their trunks, but they had lots of pine boughs at the tops. Also, they were bent across each other at their tops. They were standing in the middle of a small, open spot all by themselves. I was absolutely speechless! There were those two "coconut palms," except they were pine trees! I raced back around that little curve and yelled at everyone, "I found Dean's miracle trees!"

Everyone came and walked back around the curve with me. We all stared in wonderment at those two trees standing all by themselves in the middle of the small, open spot. Dean quickly raced over to those trees, flung himself under them, and cried again. It's been obvious since then that God had delivered Dean from his personal demons that day. As we all walked back around the little curve to our camp, we mused about how if we had just driven on around that little curve before we stopped, we would have actually gotten to the "miracle trees" that God had shown to me. Keep in mind that I was a fairly new Christian, and I didn't know much of anything about how Christianity works. Dean was just as new as I was. Carl wasn't saved yet. My sister and her husband were Christians; but they lived on the west side of the Rocky Mountain continental divide, while we all lived on the east side, in Denver. This means that God was dealing with some pretty average joes who were not schooled in Christianity. God is *not* partial; He hears and responds to anyone who asks and believes that He is listening. See Romans 2:4–11.

I just want to mention one more little miracle here before I go on to tell about the mighty miracles that God later performed regarding our son, Teddy.

While Carl, Dean, and I were at Church one Sunday morning after we were all finally saved and baptized, the church was singing and worshipping the Lord. Suddenly I saw that a blue aura was around the head of a man who was sitting about three rows ahead of us. Now, I don't believe in auras, so I tried to ignore this spectacle. But I couldn't take my eyes off of the man's head. Then God spoke quietly to me and said, "I want you to tell that man that I, God, love him."

I said, "No way!"

But God was insistent.

I turned to Carl and pointed the guy out to Carl. I told him that God wanted Carl to tell that guy up there with the blue aura around his head that God loved him. Carl said that God had never said that to him, that he didn't see any aura, and that he wasn't going to do it. So I poked Dean and told him that God wanted Dean to tell that guy up there with the blue aura around his head that God loved him. Dean said that God had never said that to him, that he didn't see any aura, and that he wasn't going to do it. At that point, I was pretty sure that I wasn't going to tell the guy anything either.

When church was over and people were filing out, that guy was walking right past us. Without warning, Dean shoved me right into that guy's arms. I was *so* embarrassed, but I finally got my mouth open and told him that God wanted me to tell him that God loved him. His eyes immediately welled up with tears, and I begged him to tell me what was wrong. He said that nothing was wrong and that it was just that God had told him several weeks ago that He wanted this guy to become a pastor. He really had trouble figuring out if that was really God speaking to him or if he was just talking to himself out of self-righteous pride. So the guy told God, if it really was God, that "if you send three strangers to tell me that You love me, then I will believe that it was really You, not myself, who was telling me to do this."

He said that two strangers had already told him that God loved him. But it had been two weeks since then, and he still hadn't gotten God's message of love from the third stranger. Then he said to me, "You are the third stranger." This is biblical; it's called putting out a fleece to make sure that it's really God talking to you. See Judges 6:36–40. All four of us—Carl, Dean, the guy, and I—were all teared up by then. So we said our goodbyes and went on home.

I prayed on the way home, "God, what would have happened if I had not given Your message to the guy?"

God answered me, "I would have found another stranger to do it, and you wouldn't have gotten to experience this miracle." He said that I would have spent a long time thinking about the incident and worrying about not obeying Him. Oh, He was so right, and I'm so glad that I gave the guy his message from God.

Our pastor had recently told the church a little story about how a person had told his friend how to get to his church. He said, "You will see a big sign with the directions to the church on it." But as his friend neared the sign, he saw a few little pigs running around under the sign. The friend got so enamored with watching the pigs that he drove right by the sign, so he never did find the directions to the church. Our pastor said, "Don't get so interested in watching the little pigs [small sins] that you miss God's directions for your life!" I'm so glad that I didn't get sidetracked by my own unbelief and thereby miss God's direction to give His message to the guy. It's a wonderful feeling to realize that you did just obey the Lord! This was a very sweet miracle.

CHAPTER 5

We have also had a couple of miracles that involved angels. The memories of them bring back great joy.

When Ted was about twelve years old, he really wanted to get a kitty. Carl and his family had always hated cats, so we had never been able to talk him into letting Ted have a cat. However, one day, Ted and I were shopping at the old Northglenn Mall. When we were about to go home, we decided to just stop in at the pet shop to enjoy looking at the animals. Ted walked down the pet-fish aisle while I went over to look at the kittens.

There was the cutest little calico kitty in the play area, and I couldn't resist just standing there and watching her play. She was so beautiful and adorable. At that time, a lady and her teenage daughter came into the store and came over to join me in watching the kitties. The daughter leaned over onto her mother's shoulder. This was amazing to me because teenagers never lean on their mothers' shoulders, especially in public!

The mother saw me enjoying that cute little calico kitty, and she said to me, "You need to buy that one." It surprised me, but I turned around to tell Ted what the lady had said to me.

Ted said, "What lady?"

When I turned back to point her out to Ted, the lady and her daughter weren't there! So then I had a conundrum. What to do?

Although Ted and I both knew that Carl had forbidden us from ever bringing a cat home, Ted joined me to look at that cute calico kitty. It wasn't long before we both knew that we had to buy that kitty. We considered that for a while but then decided to buy the kitty. We knew that we would be in trouble with Carl when we brought the kitty home, but we just had to have her, certainly after the vanishing lady had said.

When we got home and opened the front door, I put the kitty down on the floor. Carl, who was sitting in his ever-present recliner, started sputtering. The kitty spied Carl, then ran straight for him, leapt right up into his lap, and curled up on him. From that time on, Carl spent hours playing with Kitty, which was officially her name now. Kitty soon made it clear that Carl was her very favorite person in the house! Carl became putty in her paws! Surely, the lady and her daughter were angels sent to urge Ted and me to buy Kitty. He knew exactly which kitty would win Carl's heart over. In time, it became obvious that Kitty had begun to get Carl's heart to soften up. He began to get less crabby and more loving. This was truly one of God's tender miracles engineered by angels.

Ted loved kitty too, and so did I even though I was the one who wound up feeding her and changing the cat litter. We all know that this is how it goes with household pets. Mom gets to do all the work. Ted invented plenty of games to play with Kitty. The best game, though, was the one where Ted taught Kitty to ride his skateboard up and down the hallway. Kitty would try to grab the wheels as she rolled along, which made it twice as funny to watch. Kitty lived with us for sixteen fun-filled years until she passed away.

When Ted finished high school in 1999, he joined the marines. Carl and I suffered a terrible empty-nest syndrome, and it took us a long time to recover from it. However, Carl decided that now was a good time to sell our house and move to Montana. He had always wanted to move here, but Ted had always said that he wouldn't leave Denver and his friends. So when *Ted* left Denver and his friends, Carl knew that we were free to go. Carl had an aunt and uncle living here, and his brother Dean had moved here a couple of years previously. Carl asked his company for a transfer here, and they gave it to him. I wasn't the least bit happy to leave Denver either, but I was certainly going to go wherever Carl went. We had a well-established marriage of twenty-two years by then, and it was actually worth it to me even though I had to leave family and friends in Denver too.

When we got here, we found a nice affordable house after a couple of months. It was just two houses away from our new church, so we bought it and moved in. This was at the end of 1999, and we have lived here ever since. It's been another twenty-two years of an increasingly improving marriage. God constantly helped Carl and me become better people and better Christians, believers whose desires are to serve God as well as possible.

Ted at two years old   Ted as a teenager

Ted as a marine

Ted went to marine boot camp in Camp Pendleton, California. This meant that it would be thirteen weeks before we could ever get to see him again. When he graduated from boot camp, we flew to

San Diego to watch his unit's graduation ceremonies. Wow, it was so good to see Ted again! He sure looked good in his beautiful marine uniform. We got to mingle with Ted and his newfound buddies all evening long. It brought a lot of peace to our hearts at last. After boot camp, Ted was stationed at Camp Lejeune, North Carolina, for the remaining 3-3/4 years of his tour of duty. He had a great time getting to know the East Coast of America and meeting lots of new people. Ted loved and still loves the marines. He became his unit's Christian leader, he became a crack shot on the shooting range, and he earned the rank of sergeant. Ted's unit called him Sarge, and he loved that too.

When Ted was finishing his third year in basic training at Camp Lejeune, the tragedy of September 11, 2001, happened. What an awful time that was for our country. That really fired up all our heroes in the military, as we all know, and Ted was no exception to that outrage. As soon as he could, Ted re-upped in the marines for another tour of duty, which was four more years. He wanted to go with his fellow troops to Iraq to get Osama bin Laden. Thus, our next round of fearfulness began to haunt us. We leaned heavily on God's grace to carry us and get us through this fearsome time. The psalms of the Bible brought us great comfort while we struggled to remain calm and trust the Lord for the outcome of Ted's participation in war.

I put this prelude to the next set of wonderful miracles that God granted to us in order to provide context for them. I must write a little more context before I can talk about them. However, I in no way am writing about our lives to explain how special we are. Rather, I am writing about our lives to illustrate how boringly average we are. It's my intention to use our common, everyday lives to encourage other average people that they can expect to experience God's miracles in their lives too. Only believe!

GOD STILL DOES MIRACLES TODAY

Family picture of Carl, Carole, Ted, and Vinnie

Carl, Carole, and Ted; Ted is home in
Montana, on leave from the marines

CHAPTER 6

After we moved to Montana, I was very lonely. One day, as I was basking in the sunshine on our patio, I began to whine to God that He had "led me out of Egypt to a place that I didn't know." I had no idea of what to do about my loneliness. Also, I had heard that as people age, they don't do change very well. That certainly was the case for me. I had lost my ability to get out there and meet people, so everyone here was still strangers to me. After I whined to God for a bit, I remembered that I had read in our church bulletin that there was a Christian ladies' group that met at the church once a week. I thought, *Ooh, a group of older, chubby ladies. I could fit right in there!*

Then God said to me, "Get to church!"

I realized that He meant that I should go join that group. So I went and joined that group. When they handed me the workbook, I was shocked to see that it was called "Out of Egypt!" I knew then that it was God who had actually engaged me in my whinefest so that He could direct me to go to that group. It was yet another sweet miracle from God for me.

I met lots of nice ladies there, many of whom became good friends to me. We've had many really good Bible study groups together over the years, and I have been very blessed by so many of them. My loneliness disappeared pretty quickly. Furthermore, those sweet ladies helped me pray a lot for Ted's safety in Iraq every week. Carl met some wonderful Christian men at our church too. All the while, God was helping us truly mature in our Christian walks with Jesus. Peter said in 1 Peter 2:3–5 that we are to put aside our sins and instead "long for the pure milk of the Word" so that we can be "built up as a spiritual house." Also, Paul said in Hebrews 5:13–14 that we should ultimately aim for the "solid food [that] is for the mature" Christian. These passages of Scripture have so encouraged Carl and me to keep growing up in Jesus, and God has been very good to us as we've been growing.

Now I can tell you about two more of the mighty miracles that God has done for us. The first one is a miracle that involved angels. I am so excited to remember it!

When Ted re-upped in the marines, he was transferred to the Twenty-Nine Palms marine base in Southern California. He had to get special training in the art of war there. When it came nearly time for Ted to be shipped out to Iraq, Carl and I were struggling to keep trusting the Lord for Ted's safety, but we gave it our best try. Ted got a week's leave before being shipped out, but he wasn't allowed to leave California. I knew that I just had to get to California to see Ted before he left for Iraq. Carl wanted to go too, but he had to work, so he couldn't go. Besides, somebody had to earn the money for that trip!

When I got to California, I rented a car and picked Ted up at his base, and we drove back to Palm Springs in order to spend the week together. It was strikingly hot there, 108–110 degrees every day. We rented a lovely double hotel room, and we mostly just stayed in that wonderful air-conditioned room. We ordered meals in, we watched movies on the TV, we swam in the hotel swimming pool, and we had a generally good, if not sad, time. We even ventured out and saw Sonny's statue on the bench.

After a couple of days, though, we were just too bored, so we hopped in my rental car and drove on out to the Pacific Ocean and then back to Palm Springs. On the way, we saw lots of wonderful places, especially Lake Tahoe, and we had a wonderful time. But then it was time for Ted to get back to Twenty-Nine Palms so they could ship him out to Iraq, to war.

It's not hard to imagine what a horrible day that was for me when I had to drop Ted off at his base. When Ted got out of the car, I could hardly bear the pain and heartache that poured over my soul as well as the renewed fear for Ted's life. It's been about eighteen years now since that day, but I am still shaken as I write about this.

Ted wasn't afraid, though. His friends were there to greet him, and he joined them in his excitement to go off on this new adventure! Ted was still young, and he had no idea what war could do to a man. I drove off sobbing and headed back to Palm Springs to return the rental car at the airport and fly home.

I drove slowly through the bleak California desert, crying the whole way. I was so afraid that I would never see Ted again. I was also afraid to see what bad shape Carl would be in when I got home. It was 6:30 a.m., and I realized that I really needed a morning cup of coffee, but where would I get one from? "Oh, what to do? What to do?" I muttered to myself. All of a sudden, out of the blue, and all by itself, I saw a Denny's restaurant ahead. What a relief that was because I really just didn't have the strength to keep driving without a cup of coffee to help me. I pulled into the parking lot, and I saw that there were no other cars there. I got out of the car and went into the restaurant, and a waiter seated me in that empty dining room all by myself. There was only me, the waiter, and the cook in the kitchen.

I was so upset that I couldn't possibly have eaten anything, so I just ordered a cup of coffee. It was so quiet there all by myself, and then I heard some ladies talking behind me. I turned around to my right. Kitty-cornered off to the side were three pretty young ladies sitting in a booth. All three were wearing some lovely floral summer dresses, and they all had those big-brimmed, floppy straw hats on like the ones Southern belles wore. They were joyful and giggling, obviously having an all-around good time. All of a sudden, they got serious and began wondering aloud to one another how people could possibly not trust in God and give Him all their troubles. They talked about how much God loved us and how He heard us when we cried out to Him. (He hears our prayers, He is always comforting us, and He always answers all our prayers.) No, I didn't keep looking at them. I just turned away and eavesdropped on them!

Oh, how these ladies were so blessing my heart. Their words encouraged me as I was reminded that I should always go to God with all my pains and fears as well as my gratefulness to and worship of Him. I immediately began praying silently, pouring my heart out to God. The verses in Matthew 11: 28–30 came into my mind: "Come to Me all who are weary and heavy laden." Then, just as quickly as they had started, the ladies fell silent. It became eerily quiet again.

I turned back toward the ladies to see why they had so suddenly stopped laughing and talking, but there was no one there anymore! Just as I had never heard them come into the restaurant, so I had never heard them leave. Just then, the waiter came out of the kitchen to pour another cup of coffee for me. I asked him where the ladies had gone so quickly, but he said, "What ladies?"

I said, "The ladies who were sitting right there in that booth."

The waiter answered, "There were never any ladies sitting there. No one else but you has come in yet this morning." He gave me a little "Are you crazy?" look, and he walked away.

But I did not care! My heart was at peace, like Jesus said in the Matthew 11:28–30 passage: "And I will give you rest." Could those ladies have actually been angels? Of course, they were! God knew how badly I needed to be comforted, so He sent His angels to comfort me. Hebrews 1:14 says that "they...are all ministering spirits, sent out to render service for the sake of those who will inherit salvation." Hebrews 13:2 says that "some have entertained angels without knowing it."

I went back out to my car in far better shape than I had gone into Denny's with. Now I had enough strength to get back to the Palm Springs airport to turn in the rental car and fly back home to Montana. I even had words from God and some scriptures to tell Carl about to comfort him too.

Hold on now. The best miracle is coming up!

CHAPTER 7

When I got back home, Carl and I talked all about my trip and about God's miracle with angels. Carl felt a little better then too. Afterward, I called my older sister, Barbi, and told her that story. She called me back a couple of days afterward and said that my angel story had inspired her to pray even more for Ted's safety. She said that as she was praying one day, God gave her a quick yet vivid vision of Ted. He was just a little up off the ground, with wings on his heels, sort of like Cupid! Barbi said that she just knew that this vision meant that Ted was going to be just fine. I sure hoped that she was right, although I struggled with unbelief, just like everyone does. Again, though, God comforted Carl and me through a vision that He gave to Barbi.

One day, after Ted had been in Iraq for several months, we got an overseas phone call. "Oh no," we said, panicking. "This is it. It's the phone call that we have been dreading." Every day, we had been afraid that two marines were going to walk up our sidewalk to bring us that terrible news that every parent of every child who goes off to war is terrified to get. "So it's going to be given to us by phone," we sobbed.

We answered the phone. It was *Ted*! He said that he had stepped on a roadside bomb two days ago!

We yelled, "And you're still alive? Have you lost any arms or legs?"

Ted said that yes, of course, he was obviously still alive and that no, he hadn't lost any body parts! We were absolutely stunned. We begged him to explain why it had taken him two days to call us (as we had spent those two days, along with all the other days, assuming that he was still okay because no one had come to tell us differently).

We were also desperate to hear his account of this awful occurrence. Ted told us this story.

He and his marine unit of a few men were out on patrol around the little village that they were headquartered in. Ted was still the sergeant of the group, so it was his duty to walk out ahead of them to lead them. He was walking beside a mud-brick wall, and there was a tree just behind him. As he stepped down, he heard the click of an IED bomb, and he knew that he was a goner. He leaned back against the tree and called out Jesus's name, "Jesus, help me!" The bomb blew. The brick wall fell down, the tree was gone, and there was a big pit in front of Ted—but Ted was still standing! He was not injured in any way, although he did receive a TBI (traumatic brain injury). (Ted is still suffering with PTSD today, but he is slowly learning how to overcome the TBI and the PTSD with help from the VA.)

Ted said that there was a lot of smoke and dirt flying around, so he couldn't see his guys; neither could they see him. As the dust settled down, Ted came walking out of the smoke toward his guys. They couldn't believe their eyes! They said that they just expected to see "red-colored dirt left" when the smoke and dirt finally settled. At first they were even somewhat afraid that they were seeing a ghost. Then they hustled Ted off to the medical tent in the village.

Ted said that he laid, around on the cot for a while, but the medic never showed up. So, too bored, Ted got up and went back to war. He said that as he and his men walked along through some small woods, they could hear bullets zipping past them in the air and on the ground, but no one got hit. Soon they found the place where the bullets were coming from, and they "silenced them." He didn't expound on that, and we didn't ask him to. Ted's tour of duty was over shortly after that, and he was discharged and came home to Montana. He still misses his guys in his unit, and he stays in touch with them.

This is the last miracle that I am going to write about. We have experienced many miracles, large and small, and there's no need to carry on and on about them. But Ted's miracle was certainly the biggest and the best one, wasn't it? We can't explain it nor even begin to figure out how it could have ever happened. We are left to contemplate Proverbs 3:5–6: "Trust in the Lord with all your heart, and do not lean on your own understanding. In all your ways acknowledge Him, and He will make your paths straight." It's true!

POSTSCRIPT

While Ted was in the marines, he always came to Montana when he was on leave to stay with us and learn about Montana. He loved seeing the several cousins that he has here as well as his aunts, uncles, and so forth. However, when Ted finally got out of the marines, he went back to Denver to live. That was hard for us, but God has faithfully helped us to get through it. Ted brings his family to Montana to visit us every summer, and that is a wonderful thing.

Ted got married in due time, had two beautiful children, moved to the southern foothills of Denver, and established his own business, which he named Victory Mechanical. He named his company this name because of his many victories from Jesus—you know, "Victory in Jesus, my Savior forever."

Once again, I want to reiterate that this family is just a group of average joes. We can make no claim of being anything greater than this. We are not so special that God makes extraordinary efforts to make His miracles happen for us. What we are, though, is a family of believers in our miracle-making God. We have learned to trust Him in the worst of times because we know that He will handle our problems, heal our wounds, teach us how to obey Him even better, and grant us a miracle when He sees that we need one. When it's time to go home, God will take us.

This can be anyone's life experience if they just step out in faith before God and believe He will willingly meet all their needs. They can live an everyday life that is full of God's extraordinary miracles. In Matthew 6:31–34, Jesus said that God will take care of us. Verse 33 says that we must "seek first His kingdom and His righteousness, and all these things shall be added to you." The following three steps are worth following: (1) We must step out in faith before God will step out to meet us with His miracles, (2) God proves His trustworthiness to us when we first prove our trustworthiness to Him, and (3) God blesses our obedience to Him. None of these things are hard to do. They are serious things, though, and they must be taken seriously. As I have said, I wrote this little book in order to encourage all believers to pray, believing at all times. Read John 16:33. *Amen.*

Helena, Montana

SCRIPTURE LIST

Old Testament
Genesis 1:1
Genesis 1:14
Judges 6:36–40
Proverbs 3:56
Malachi 3:6

New Testament	
Matthew 6:31–34	Acts 2:17–18
Matthew 7:7	Acts 19:11–12
Matthew 11:28–30	Romans 2:4–11
Matthew 20:21	1 Corinthians 12:1
Mark 9:23	Hebrews 1:14
Mark 16:17–18	Hebrews 5:13–14
Luke 11:9	Hebrews 13:5–6, 8
John 15:3	James 5:16
John 16:33	1 Peter 2:3–5
	1 John 3:21–22

All scriptures are from the New American Standard Bible. It's the most accurate Bible translation.

ABOUT THE AUTHOR

Carole Arnold is a homemaker. Her husband, Carl, is a retired union pipefitter. Carole has two grown sons plus three grown stepchildren and four grandchildren. She and Carl have been married for forty-five years. They have been born-again believers for forty years. They live happily in Helena, Montana. Their son, Ted, and Carole's son, Vinnie, live in Denver, Colorado.